Mindful Parenting

40 Mindful Moments to Share with Your Child

Rachel Hawkes

Contents

Hello, from an imperfect parent!

Yes, I'm with you — seeking to become not just a better parent but also, develop tools to share with our kids. It's hard being a parent but we are also painfully aware of how much pressure our children are under.

More tests, increased peer pressure and of course the joy of social media!

How can we help them and take a step forward on the long road that is being a parent?

Mindfulness – yes I know you have heard all about it! It's sitting in a lotus position with super bendy legs, in some sort of state of bliss, possibly elevated several inches from the floor! Mmm, or maybe not. For me, mindfulness is about being in 'the moment' – one that we can share with our children and more importantly allow them to find for themselves.

If you want to go down the rabbit hole that is research on 'mindfulness' (and believe me, I've been there), then go for it. This book is about providing simple tools and techniques for you to be able to introduce mindfulness into your home. There will be plenty of tips and tricks, all together they form a complete package of skills you can pick from.

Parenting

I couldn't wait to be a parent! It took time but I finally got there and..... oh my I realised (very quickly) that it was going to take a whole new set of skill sets! I knew that parenting was going to be challenging but thought it was just about lack of sleep and juggling time. Now – 12 years on I realise how naïve I was.

Luckily, I had been practising yoga for several years and when I first started classes I was introduced to mindfulness by an amazing Yoga teacher. Through a great deal of patience (on her part), to slowly enable me to find some moments of calm at the end of a class.

Moments of calm. That's what I now needed as a new parent. The ability to be able to stop, take a breath and enjoy the moment. If you are reading this book, I am hoping that you are also looking for those same moments. For you and your children.

This booked is aimed at you. The parent that knows they do not have all the answers. Who can see that both; as a parent and an individual we need to be able to appreciate the joy when it is in the smallest detail. Of those early artistic efforts put up on the fridge or the hug before running into school.

I wrote this with all of us in mind. To be able to just take a precious moment and saviour it. For our children to be able to see the joy in a moment and have the tools to be able to create it for themselves.

As parents we can feel overwhelmed by the sheer amount of stuff to do, alongside ensuring that our children are not just healthy, well rounded, academically successfully but also HAPPY! What if, together we were able to find more happy moments?

This is meant as an introduction into how, often without any other props, gimmicks or apps you can simply begin to be more present with your children. How they can learn from you with easy techniques that will enable them to also enjoy, develop and grow as the individuals that they are.

Enjoy the journey
X
Rachel

Mindfulness
– a definition

'Bringing your awareness to the present moment'

Well, that is my way of thinking of it. There are lots of more complex definitions out there but sometimes simplicity is key.

Easy to read, with techniques that are simple to implement. That is how this book is structured. I have taken some of the many known techniques of Mindfulness and broken them down into separate chapters.

You can simply work through one chapter, or dip in and out of different ones. The key is to find ways that work for you and your family! If you have a real live wire, then maybe start with some scarf breathing. Getting them up and going first is often the key to grounding them after. We are not looking to create passive, instruction followers. Mindfulness is all about engagement. You just need to find what will engage your kids.

I hope that the variety of practices will give you some tools to find some Mindful Moments with your children.

Mindfulness
Basics

So, before we get into the various ways you can be 'mindful' let's talk about the basics. What are the things you need to be aware of, or do before you begin bringing mindfulness into your life?

I have split this down into some of the key 'basics' that can help you and your family make this an integral part of your lives, easily and without much fuss.

1. Anytime, anywhere – firstly, do not get too hung up in sitting in the right position, eyes closed with tranquility around you. Often the best Mindful Moments are in the craziness of a park or running down a hill. These basics are here for you, as you and your child develop these Mindful skills but really the art of the moment is to be able to embrace it, wherever it may be!

2. Breathing position – It is a good idea to impart the basic understanding of how the breath works. How the breath comes into the body and out. The language you use will be down to the age of your child. For the younger children, keep it simple with and 'in' and 'out'. For the older children you may want to use 'inhale' and 'exhale'.

3. It is also important that the chest is open so as much air can get into the body as possible. You may want to have them start by lying down, or if sitting up, then maybe explain that when they sit up nice and tall more air can get into the body. Again, use the terms that you think your child will understand. Take your time with this one, children can get very caught up in doing this 'right' rather than just being 'aware'.

4. I would also like to cover 'grounding'. This is having a connection to the ground physically. It can have a great effect on any mindful activity. This simply means that some part of your body is in contact with the ground. If you are sitting it can be your feet, if you are lying down it can be the whole body. Again, this will not work for all practices but if you can have it in mind it can really help with your child's connection.

5. Positions for focus work. You can sit or lie down with your child. I often have us holding hands to feel more of a connection. It is important to stress that comfort is the key. Especially with younger children we do not need to become rigid on the position they are in, or if they stay still. In fact, for some children with ADHD or other learning issues it maybe too challenging for them to remain still

for the duration of the exercise. Therefore, it is essential that each child is allowed to find their own comfort level.

6. Start with some of the smaller exercises, mindfulness takes time to practice and you do not want you, or your child to become bored.

7. This book comes with a selection of techniques, these allow for a variety of learning needs however each element of each section can be utilised on its own, or put together.

8. This book is designed to be interchangeable. Each parent delivering sessions will be able to 'create' a practice suitable for their children. For example; if you have a child who is scared of hot air balloons you can simple 'swap' that breathing techniques for one of the another technique's.

9. Be creative, allow your children to bring their own creativity to these sessions. They are an ideal space to allow open imagination, sessions are far more engaging when this happens.

10. There is no '**right or wrong**'. Intent is the key underpinning these sessions. As long as children are actively participating then everything else can be worked on. If they breathe out instead of in, or cannot 'picture the beach' in a visualisation, then it does not matter. These practices are here to provide tools for helping with many mental and emotional issues, not to feed any current anxieties.

11. Before beginning delivery of any of these practices, I've found that it is really helpful to have a little chat that covers these 'Mindfulness Basics". A

simple discussion on 'what is mindfulness' between the you and child would ensure that time is not spent during the mindful sessions answering these questions.

12. If your child has additional needs, I have tried to carefully cater for aspects of emotional, social, developmental and learning needs in this book. However, as a parent, maybe you can spend some preparation time before delivery to ensure these the techniques you are using that day will suit them. Mindfulness can be an amazing tool to use with many of the additional needs facing our children today.

Breathing
Techniques

1. Balloon Breath
2. Scarf Breathing
3. Blow the bubbles
4. Flower breathing
5. Teddy Bear breath
6. Ping Pong breath
7. Feather breath
8. Hot Air Balloon
9. Stone Breathing
10. Counting the breath

1. Balloon Breath (not for those with dislike or fear balloons – however you can use imaginary balloons not real ones). Although this can be a fun way of teaching breath work with a balloon, it also works really well with imaginary balloons.

Sitting in a kneeling position in a circle have your arms in front of you at shoulder height and your hands touching, palms together. Now imagine your arms are a giant balloon. Using our breath we are going to inflate and deflate our balloon. So backs are straight, chest is open, shoulders are down and back.

This is the starting point for all breath work. In order for our lungs to get the biggest amount of air we need to ensure that our chest is open and we are not slouching. Now as you take a deep breath in take your arms out to the side as wide as you can. Stop when you can't take in any more air, then as you breathe out bring the arms back to together again. Now this time take the arms up a little higher and again as you breath in, take the arms out to the side and as you breathe out you bring the arms back to the centre with the hands touching.

Again repeat, this time start by taking the arms right over your head, as you breath in bring the arms out and then as you breathe in bring them back to the starting position over your head. With palms together breath in and as you breathe out bring the hands down, palms together until your hands are level with your heart.

2. Scarf Breathing – This is a great way of working with breath with younger children as the focus is not on technique but awareness. This can also include individual, partner and team work.

With a selection of scarfs in the centre get every child to pick a scarf. Now everyone stand up and then take your scarf above your head. You have to try and keep the scarf from landing on the ground but you can only use your breath! (Ensure that everyone had plenty of room). You can join your child or children in this activity. If you have more than 1 child it is a great game to get them working together. Try working together to see how long you can keep the scarf in the air.

This is a method of using the breath without being focused on the 'how'. We do not need to explain too much about the technique but can explain how it is our 'out – exhale' that keeps the scarf up. We can then go through in/ out – inhale/ exhale. You can choose the language that you think will fit for the age of your children. Then work on small breath, big breath, what happens if we use lots of little breaths or one big breath?

Variations – Placing the Scarf over our face and seeing the movement from our breath – this is often a good starting point for this exercise.

Using more than one scarf – the weight means we need to work harder to move the scarfs?

You can always bring in other educational aspects, such as counting, colours, and shapes

3. Bubble Breathing – This is a great exercise for all ages and again is a good introduction into breath work. Either a bubble machine can be used or a specific children can be 'chosen' to blow bubbles from pots.

The aim is to move the bubbles using only your breath. Again you can explain why the 'breath is important' and how it works (inhale/ exhale – in/ out, Shallow/ deep breath).

Variations – All the family together with a bubble machine
Partners – One blowing the other chasing, taking turns

Teams – One blowing and the other chasing, taking turns.

This is also great for the hand to eye coordination as many younger children will still love to run around and pop the bubbles with their hands! Who doesn't love chasing bubbles?

With any of the above exercises it is important to pause part through to ensure that it does not get frenzied but also to be able to change the breath work, small shallow breathes to long deep breathes, one big breath or lots of small breathes. Taking the time to notice how the body feels using the breath in these different ways.

At the end of each exercise it would be great to allow some time to reflect with your child on how they notice the difference between using the breath in different ways.

Children need time after each exercise to process the activity and be able to see how it felt in their bodies. It is this growing awareness that provides them with the skills to be able to take these techniques and use them in different ways but also to be able to see that although it is fun it also teaches them what their breath is, how it works and how it affects changes in their bodies when they use it in different ways.

4. Flower Breathing – This can be used at any time of year but is not suitable for children with hayfever. You can always improvise by using some tissues and a lavender oil (this does not usually affect hayfever sufferers). Ensure that there are enough flowers/ tissues for each of your children. This is a great exercise to bring nature into your home, you can then introduce this topic in a tangible way that all the children can engage with.

Each child will simply hold the flower or tissue while in a sitting position. We start by taking a breath in through the nose and out through the mouth, in and out, in and out. Then we can hold the tissue/ flower up to our nose and smell, using the technique of breathing in through our nose and out through the mouth. Repeat this for several breathes asking the children to close their eyes if they are comfortable.

Now we can ask everyone what they smelt or how they felt. Could they smell the smell through just their nose or could they also almost taste it as they breathed out? If a child cannot think of anything ask them about the flower, is it small, large, pretty, bright, colourful etc. We can then open a discussion about how your body felt as you were breathing in, did you use a short breath or breathe in deeply? How did it feel if you had your eyes closed? Did you think that the smell was stronger or just the same?

Variations – this can be done as a whole family on in partners or teams.

You can just use tissues and essential oils instead of flowers – choosing some oils that are safe to use with children such as Lavender, Camomile, tea tree, Lemon, Bergamot etc. Children can keep the tissues if they want to, they can be put in bed as if using Lavender or Camomile they are great for relaxation.

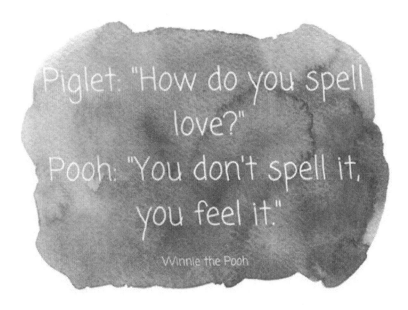

Piglet: "How do you spell love?"
Pooh: "You don't spell it, you feel it."

Winnie the Pooh

5. Teddy Bear Breath – This is more suitable for the younger children (under about 8 years old), or those children with sensory or attention difficulties. Ask your child to bring their favourite cuddly toy.

In our starting position, where children are lying down on their backs on their beds or the floor, we ask them to place their toy on their tummy. They can keep their hands on top of the toy on their tummy, or place them either side of their body. Closing our eyes, we are going to start a breath in through the nose and out through the mouth, in and out, in and out. Now I want you to think about your cuddly toy on your tummy, and as you next breath in focus your breath into your tummy and feel your toy rise up slightly.

Now as you breathe out, think of the air leaving your tummy and see if you can notice how your tummy now falls a little. You are making your cuddly toy move up and down just using the power of your breath! Do not force it, just be gentle thinking of in (tummy rises), out (tummy falls). Keep to your own pace, not to fast or too slow. Not holding your breath but keeping the in and out a slow and steady pace, in and out, in and out. Just start to breath normally and keep your mind thinking of your cuddly toy (name it if it helps).

Notice now the rest of your body, do you feel heavier on the floor? Are you aware that your legs and arms feel heavy? Does your mind feel calm? Do your hands feel warm? Just notice these things going on inside of you. Now take your awareness to the rest of the room, does it also feel different? Stay in this position until you notice that your child is starting to fidget or lose focus. Now taking a deep breath in, wiggle your fingers and toes and then breathe out and open your eyes. Roll to one side and give your toy and cuddle, then slowly come up to sitting.

Variations – Older kids can always use other props that are used in some of the other exercises such as the scarfs or feathers.

Again ensure that when you come back to sitting you allow time for the children to process how they felt so that they can replicate the exercise at any time.

6. Ping Pong Breath – this is a great stand-alone exercise or can be used as a 'game' element. You will need a straw and a ping pong ball, your child lies on the floor and needs to move the ball via blowing through the straw. As you can imagine, there are many ways to add variety into this. You can set up goals, playing ping pong football, one person on one side with a partner opposite. You can set up small teams, one ball but also still using the goals, the players then need to score a goal. An obstacle course is

also fun, place 2 -3 objects on the floor and the children need to negotiate their ball around the objects. This is always fun, more so for the slightly older children as they are more aware of the technique need to blow through the straw. For the younger children, I would start with just getting used to blowing through the straw. Using hair is a good place to start – 'can you move Mummy's hair just using the power of your breath through the straw?'

7. **Feather Breath** – this works with almost any age. You will need a selection of feathers. Again it works well as either an individual task or in pairs or teams. The aim is to keep the feather from landing on the floor. Variations can be; starting with the feather on your hand, then up high, then working in pairs to keep the feather in the air. A great tip is to use a variety of sized feathers; this can

add to the engagement of discussion at the end of the session 'was it easier to keep the small or the large feather in the air' etc. We have listed suppliers in our Resource section, at the end of the book.

8. Hot Air Balloon – This uses a combination of movement and creativity to allow the children to notice how their whole body is used when working with the breath. Start in a sitting position, back straight with the chest open ready to take a breath. Now as you breathe in, slowly come to standing, in time with the breath. As you breath out, run around the room, just like a balloon that has been deflated. Variations include; staying in a sitting position, as you breath in slowly take your arms out to the side and up overhead. As you breath out bring them back to rest in your lap. This is a calmer, version and can be a good

level to start with. Also it would be a great activity to use as a brain break in between homework. Or you can take this outside and make it far more dynamic, a way to expel lots of energy before you start with a more focused technique.

You cannot find peace by avoiding life.

Virginia Wolfe

9. Stone Breath – for any age and a great one to use with all the family, if you are including them in sessions or activities. Each child will need a 'special' object – we often use a crystal which we call our 'mindful stones' or 'magic stones'. The importance of the object is that it fits into the hand and is tactile. Part of bringing this into the session is allowing each child to choose – they need to select or have their own stone. It can be a great family activity to 'find' an object, or a weekend mission? Often children have a 'collection' of shells or fossils or just items they have picked up. The key is that they are part of the process. If you are using a collection of stones, then take the time for each child to carefully choose which stone they wish to use. They need to choose one that they like and feel a connection to.

Once they all have one, everyone is to lie down, in a comfortable position. Holding the stone in their hand, take them through the usual basics, that you covered earlier. Get comfy, close your eyes and take a breath in then out. The aim of using the stone/ shell is to have a point of focus, this is a tangible object that they can feel. It allows for greater concentration and less distraction. Start by using the senses: – "how does the stone feel in your hand?", "is it smooth, or rough?", "is it hot or cold?", "what about the size of the stone?", "is it Small?" "does it fit in your palm of your hands?"," What about the shape?" "Is it round, or maybe on odd shape?" "Does it have any edges or rough areas?" This brings the focus onto the tangibles and then you can start being more creative "what colour is your stone?", they can always look again to check. "Do you like this colour?'' "is this your favourite colour, or perhaps not a colour you even recognise?" "Picture the colour in your mind, does the colour make you feel a certain way? Maybe you feel really calm when you picture it, or perhaps it reminds you of someone or a place you have been or something you own."

This aspect can continue if the children are still actively listening. If they are getting restless, move on. "So how about you move your stone around, first from one hand to the other. Does it feel different in your other hand? Have you noticed if your stone has changed temperature? Maybe it is hotter than before, or perhaps cooler? What about moving the stone between your fingers, does it feel different? Now, just hold your stone in one hand, place that hand on your tummy. Think about the stone, gently resting on your tummy and as you breath, feel how your hand and the stone rise up, then when you breath out, feel how it lowers again."

Come out of the exercise as soon as you can feel interest is waning. So, wiggles your toes, slowly open your eyes, roll to one side and then come back up to sitting. You can have some amazing discussions from this – if you have time they can show their stone to a friend and discuss what they liked about it. Word of warning – they can become very attached to their 'mindful stone'! Again, as a family activity this can be used at any time. It really is a great fidget toy!

10. Counting the breath – this can be as simple or complicated as you need. However, when starting with counting it works to build up the practice, so start with some simple techniques first. Also, with your younger children, be aware that you are only introducing focused breath work. I would not look to start breath counting with any child under the age of at least 5 or 6. They can often hold their breath or force it, either of which slightly defeats the object.

So, starting small and again in our beginning postures, either sitting or lying down if the space allows. Start with the eyes closed and then you can explain that we will be working on a breathing technique that helps us to focus on how work with our breath. "We are going to count our breath in and out, as we breath in we count for 1, then out 1, in for 1, out for 1, now making the breath longer in, 1,2 and then out 1,2. Now extending that breath to the count of 3, breath in 1,2,3 now out 1, 2, 3. Keeping at just the count for 3 we are going to repeat that 4 times." Count through every time, so that you maintain their focus and everyone is working at the same pace. Once you finish the cycle you ask everyone to just breath normally. For children under 7 I would advise that you only do a small count of no more than 3, for the older children maybe a count up to 5. Be aware of your child, if they appear to be holding their breathe or struggling, then always go back to a normal breath.

Variations: Count 1,2,3 then hold the in breath, then out 1,2,3. Repeat up to 4 times. As above but then hold the out breath as well. Again repeat up to 4 times. Count to 10 with the breath – 1 in, 2 out, 3 in, 4 out, 5 in, 6 out, 7 in, 8 out, 9 in and 10 out. This is a good exercise to gain pace and calm, also the number 10 is enough for them to engage without then being bored. You can also add a hold at the end of the inhale and the exhale on this one, so 1 in, Hold, 2 out, hold etc. This will slow the whole exercise down even further but again they will need to have built up some practice beforehand, otherwise they can hold the breath for too long.

The counting of breath can be very powerful but you will need to remain with your eyes open throughout to ensure that your child is not forcing their breath. Also, as soon as they begin to lose interest stop. You will need to start small with this one. Only do one counting practice at a time. You will see from the list above that the variety of ways you can use it is huge but remember, kids get bored easily.

Visualisations

1.   Anxiety beach
2.   Colour bubble
3.   Colour Breathe
4.   Mindful stone
5.   Body scan
6.   My garden
7.   Magic carpet
8.   Box of cares
9.   Time with Nature
10.   Singing bowl

These 10 exercises are all what are known as 'guided visualisations'. Each one is a script that you can use to paint a picture for your child. Some will work better than others, depending of course on your child! Feel free to add in, take out, change any element you wish. They are here as a base for you to try out.

Many people feel awkward reading out to their children, but hopefully you will see that this is just like any reading you do with your child. If you make it engaging, then you will have their full attention.

Personally, guided visualisations are my favourite form of mindful practice. Listening to another voice describing a place, time or object provides great focus. For some children you will see how they are painting that picture in their head, for others they may just fidget. Stay with it, these can be pretty powerful.

Through visualisations you can connect to many emotional aspects of your child. Anxiety Beach is a great one for dealing with any worries, you picture throwing away your worry or trouble. A great tool to provide for any child. Or there is the connection of the Body Scan, bringing the attention to their own body, great for those growing children who can often feel disconnected to what is happening to them.

Have a read through, pick 1 or 2 that you think your child will like and give it a go. Also you can head to the website, http://www.buddhabuddies.co.uk/rescources where I shall be adding audio versions that you can simply download. That way you can always play the audio of a visualisation that your child is drawn to.

With these, you would just pick one. I would not do more than 1 at a time. Take your time when you are reading them out, just as when you read a story, pace is really important. Give your child time to think and picture your story. They will connect and you both will enjoy some more 'mindful moments'

1. Anxiety Beach

Picture yourself on a beach, full of pebbles. As you walk along this beach take your gaze to the pebbles under your feet, bend and pick one of the pebbles. Imagine in your mind eye what your pebble looks like (is it small, large, rough, smooth, what colour is it?)

Walking toward the shore I want you to think about anything that may have been troubling you? It could be something at home or school, a friendship that you are having problems with or school work that you are finding difficult. This trouble or worry is not something you have to keep; we are going to 'throw away this worry'.

Picture the pebble as your worry. Whatever it was is now inside the pebble that you are holding. As you walk towards the shore, look out at the sea in front of you, now holding onto your worry pebble I want you to picture throwing the pebble as far as you can out to sea. As you watch the pebble hit the water, imagine your worry is sinking to the bottom of the sea, just like the pebble. Let the worry go, feel it leaving your mind as the pebble sinks further and further to the bottom of the sea. You can no longer see your pebble, it has been 'thrown away', sinking to the bottom of the sea. Imagine your pebble, picture how it is sinking into the sea, deeper it goes until you can no longer picture it at all.

Now take a moment to think about how you now feel? Do you feel lighter knowing that you can easily cast these worries away? You can come back to this spot any time you need. It is a place that is just for you. All you need is your own imagination to return here whenever you need to.

Anytime you feel anxious or worried you can come to this shore, pick a pebble and throw it, and your worry away.

For now, we are going to walk away from the shoreline, along the beach and start to bring our awareness back to this room. Take a breath in through your nose and breathe out through your mouth. Wiggles your fingers and your toes. Take another breathe in and stretch your arms overhead, imagine you are trying to make your body as long as you can. Stretch through the arms, fingers, legs and toes. Now when you breath out bring your arms back to your side and relax the body. Slowly open your eyes. Roll to one side and slowly come back up to sitting.

2. Colour Bubble

(For those children with Autism or Sensory Issues, coloured scarfs or feathers can be used at the beginning of this exercise. Allow each child to pick his/ her colour but choosing a scarf or feather that they can then hold for the duration of the visualisation.)

Lying or sitting comfortably, close your eyes. Now take a breath in through the nose and breathe out through your mouth. Again, breath in and out, in and out. Feel yourself become heavier with each breathe out and just focus on my voice. As you relax imagine a giant bubble surrounding your body. Think of the bubbles from a bubble machine, what if it could make one big enough for you whole body to fit into? Think of your body fitting into a bubble that big. It is all around you and your body is sitting right in the middle. This bubble is safe and all full of air, you can just sit right there and gaze all around.

In your mind I want you to picture a colour. The first one that pops into your head (if using feathers/ scarfs, then think of the colour of the object in your head). What about if you could fill your bubble with this colour? Let's start by using our breath, as you breathe in imagine your colour starting to change the colour of the air in your bubble, starting in front of you, then to the left, then the right, now underneath you.

Your bubble is slowly changing colour and you are surrounded in your very own, safe colour bubble. Nothing outside of the bubble can touch you but you are safe to leave your bubble anytime – it is one you have created. Think of your colour – is it light or dark, soft or bright. Can you change the depth of the colour? Maybe it is a gentle light colour but as you focus you can make the colour become deeper? Or perhaps it is perfect just as it is. Just take the time to enjoy the calm feeling of sitting in your colour bubble. A place where no outside thoughts, or things to do, or people can bother you. This is somewhere that sits in your own mind, a safe place you can always come to. (Let your child stay there as long as they need, as soon as they start to become restless you can begin to bring them out of the visualisation).

Now as we need to leave our bubble soon we are going to let go of the colour first. So slowly as you next breath, out imagine the colour floating away, out of the bubble. Watch as is leaves the bubble and dissolves into the air, slowly and peacefully. We now need to bring our minds back to the room so allow the side of your bubble to get bigger and bigger until it finally disappears. Now you are back in the room and we are going to have a lovely wiggle of our fingers and toes as we slowly open our eyes. Take a breath in and out and then roll to one side before sitting-up.

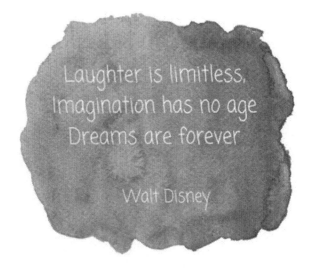

Laughter is limitless.
Imagination has no age
Dreams are forever

Walt Disney

3. Colour Breath

(This can be used on its own or with the colour bubble – again for those children that need to a prop such as a scarf or feather can be picked before the exercise)

As you sit, calmly in your colour bubble, imagine breathing in the colour surrounding you. With every in breath you are spreading your colour from your toes all the way up to your head. You can fill your whole body with this colour.

Sitting or lying comfortably take a breath in through the nose and out through the mouth. Again, in and out, in and out, feel your body relax and become heavier against the mat. When you are ready I would like you to picture a colour, maybe from something you are holding or a colour that you love, or even one you are wearing. Just pick something that feels right to you now. It might not be your favourite colour but for some reason today it is the colour your mind is thinking of. That is alright, there is no right or wrong, just allow your mind to choose without thinking too much about it. Have you got the colour in your mind yet? Did you know that colour can be a great way of allowing your mind to relax? Colour is everywhere but we do not always appreciate its beauty.

So today we are going to use that colour you are thinking of to relax our bodies and minds. Picture your colour, now imagine that you can change the air in front of you to the colour. When you breathe in you are imagining that coloured air coming into your body, through your nose, into your chest, then tummy. As you breath out the colour stays in you, this colour is going to spread through your whole body, just using your own breath you are going to fill your body with this gorgeous coloured air.

What is you were made of glass, can you picture how this filling with your colour would look. With each breath in more and more of your body fills with your colour. When your body is full of colour, from head to toe think about how you feel? Do you feel all parts of your body, does it feel funny? Do you feel lighter, like you could float away or heavier as if you are sinking into your mat? Everyone will feel different as we all choose different colours. Even if we have both picked blue, there are so many shades of each colour that we will all picture something unique – that's how amazing our minds are.

Feel that connection to your body and that colour, and how it makes you feel right now in this moment. Although your mind is busy working it feels calm and relaxed, as you are able to give your mind and body time to connect. You can enjoy this time of connection and maybe later today you can think again of this colour and what it means to you. For now, we have to come back to the room, so we are slowly going to allow the body to let go of the colour. Using our breath as we breathe in and out the colour is going to fill the space around us and the gently fade away. When your colour has gone you are going to wiggle your fingers and toes, roll to your side and slowing come to sitting.

4. Mindful Stone

Pass the treasure box of stones (or pebbles from the beach – something that can fit into the hand easily and is a natural object) to your child while explaining that they need to pick a stone. Not just any stone, but one that they really like.

Getting into our mindful position – we are going to sit or lay down making sure we are comfortable. Shuffle around until your body is at ease. Close your eyes and breath in through your nose and out through your mouth, in and out, in and out. Now allow your body to relax and focus on my voice as today we are going to work with a mindful stone.

You picked a stone from the treasure box, can you feel the stone in your hand? Hold it in the palm/ centre of one hand, how does it feel? Does it fit easily into your hand? Is it small or large, rough or smooth. What shape is it, round or long, shaped or sharp? Now roll the stone between your fingers, how does that feel? Do you want to just hold the stone in your hand or move it between your fingers or even between each hand. Do whatever feels right, making sure to keep contact with the stone all the time. Now what about the temperature, is your stone cool, warm or hot? Has it changed since you picked it? Is it changing now as you think about it? Just take a few moments and focus on your stone, maybe think about why you picked it? Was it the colour or the shape or the size?

Now place the hand or hand holding the stone onto your tummy and think about your breath. As you breath in and out feel the stone on your tummy. Can you feel the stone against you? Does it feel different having it on you as you breathe? Again take a moment to picture the stone in your hand as you simply breathe.

Time to bring our awareness back into the room, so slowly start to focus back from your stone and be aware of being in the room. As you breath in place your stone on your tummy, as you breathe out wiggle your fingers and toes. Now picking up your stone, roll to one side and slowly come back to sitting.

Later can you discuss why you picked that stone, or write it in a journal or talk about it with someone at home. I wonder if you will pick the same stone next time or a different one? There are lots of amazing things about these mindful stones and these can be discussed in more depth at another mindful session or maybe on the way to school. This can be a great introduction into energy and/ or chakras if you want to introduce this to your children.

5. Body Scan

This is a great one to do if you can get your kids to lie down. This is all about using the body as the focus tool, so being in a lying down position can really help them relax as you talk them through. We are going to focus on our own body today. Using our breath, we will work from our toes to our head and 'check in' to see how our body feels. Take a nice breath in through the nose and out through the mouth, and again. Now starting with your toes, breath in and screw up your toes as tight as you can.

As you breath out, relax the toes and give them a wiggle. Now onto your lower leg, breath in and try to tighten the muscles in your lower legs, breath out and relax. Up to the top of the legs, breath in tighten as much as you can, now breath out and relax. Letting all the muscles of the legs feel floppy. Now how about those lovely bottoms (expect lots of giggles!), breath in and tighten them, now breath out and let the muscles go.

Our tummy's turn next, breath in and imagine how tight you can get your tummy to feel, now breath out and let those muscles go. Our shoulders can also do with some attention to think about bringing your shoulders down, feel how the back in connecting to the floor underneath you.

Breath in, feel the shoulder blades against the floor and breath out and relax. Take your thoughts to your hands. Breath in and form your hands into a really tight fist, as if you were trying to squeeze something really tight. Now breath out and relax that grip, wiggle those fingers and now let them rest gently on the floor. Thinking of your right arm, breath in and tighten the arm so that you can feel it almost lift off the floor.

Now breath out and relax the arm, letting it rest lightly on the floor. The same for the left side, breath in, tighten and then breath out and relax. All the way to our faces now. Think of your jaw, have your mouth open very slightly and feel your tongue able to move in your mouth. Make sure your eyes are closed, not squeeze them closed really tight, now breath and relax. Picture your eyes just resting behind your eyelids.

Taking a lovely breath in, think about how your whole body now feels. In your mind can you picture yourself lying there? Are you able to feel how all of your body is feeling? Does it make you feel heavier? Or maybe lighter? Is there a part of you that feels different from the rest of you?

Take a moment and really think about your body from the toes to the tip of your nose. (Let the children rest in this position for 2-3 minutes if possible, if they are starting to fidget then make the time shorter).

Now we need to bring our awareness back to the room and the rest of the class. Slowly as you take a breath in take your arms overhead and have a lovely big stretch. All through the fingers and the toes. As you breath out take the arms back to your sides. Open your eyes, roll to one side and begin to sit up.

6. My Garden

We are going to visit a special place today, all in our minds. So time to get comfy. I would like you to think of a really beautiful garden, maybe one you have visited before, or even your own garden! It does not have to be a real place, it could be one that as you close your eyes and think 'garden' your imagination is already painting a picture in your head.

This is a lovely, warm Summer garden with plenty of grass and trees. In your mind look down and your feet, they are bare and you are standing on cool green grass. Feel the grass between your toes, squish your toes so you can really feel the grass. Now, looking up and around I want you to think of all the different senses we use every day. You can see your garden, the colours and the plants, trees and even birds. Can you think about what sounds you might be hearing? Is it the call of the birds, bees buzzing, the wind rustling through the leaves of the trees?

Take a moment and really look around, think of all the things you can see and hear. What about the things you can smell, touch and taste? Maybe there is a fruit tree there. What fruit would you want to have in your garden? A bright apple, a juicy peach or a scrummy pear? Look into your garden and see a tree with your favourite fruit on it. Maybe it is a tree of your imagination – not even something that exists. This is your garden, so it can be whatever you want it to be. Walk towards your tree, still feeling the grass under your feet. As you near the tree you can see the fruit, they are hanging from the branches. Reach out and take one. Bring it up to your nose, what does it smell like?

Can you imagine it? What about the feel of the fruit in your hand? Now take a lovely big bite of your fruit. Is it crunchy or juicy? Is it sweet or sour? Think of what this fruit would taste like, just picked from your very own garden. Now think about how you have used all your senses to really bring your garden to life in your mind.

Take a moment and look around, thinking of all the things that you can smell, taste, touch, see and hear. Isn't it amazing what your mind and imagination can do! You can come back to this special place anytime, for it is in your own mind. If you need to find a moment to relax or be calm, then you can simply close your eyes and come back to this – your very own garden. Maybe you would like to spend a few moments here, sitting under your fruit tree and thinking of how warm and calm it is. (take as much time as you need with this one, sometimes the more often they are taken to this place, the longer they will spend)

It is time to leave our lovely garden's, so take one last look around and then take a deep breath in, slowly breathe out. Now wiggle your toes and open your eyes. Roll to one side and come back to sitting.

When you talk you are
only repeating what you
already know,
but when you listen
you may learn something new.

Dalai Lama

7. Magic Carpet

This can be a lovely visualisation to use before bedtime, and works really well if they are already in bed and you can sit by their side. We are going to be really working with our imaginations today as we take a trip on a magic carpet! So why don't you start by closing your eyes and taking a nice deep breath in and out. You can shift around until you are feeling comfy and just relax as we take this trip together. You are walking through a lovely grass field, the sky is blue and the sun is shining. It is a beautiful day and you are able to look around you and see how blue the sky is, how warm the air, you can even hear the birds singing in the trees.

Walking forward you see the strangest sight. A large gorgeous carpet is on the ground; it is brightly coloured with tassels all around the edges. What could this carpet be doing in the middle of a field? Look down at the carpet, what colours do you see? Does it have a design or a picture on it?

You walk onto the carpet, it is so soft under your feet that you decide to have a lie down and relax. This though, is no ordinary carpet but a magic carpet that can take you anywhere that your mind can imagine! All you need to do is picture somewhere and this carpet can safely take you there! So let's all imagine a beautiful castle, its walls are bright and it has turrets with flags flying. As we start to form this picture in our minds, our carpet begins to rise from the ground. Slowly at first, you can feel it rising but know that the carpet (as it is magic) will keep you safe, it feels very strong under your body. You are now flying through the sky, imagine that you are opening your eyes and the first thing you see are birds, flying right by the side of you!

How amazing, you could almost reach out and touch them. High in the sky you are up amongst the clouds, looking like giant cotton wool. You take a peak further and there amongst the clouds you begin to see the tall towers of the castle. The flags are flying in the breeze and you see that the walls of the castle begin to get clearer as you get near. The walls are so bright that the sun seems to shine off them, they are white and clear against the blue sky.

Your carpet begins to circle over the tall turrets of the castle and you notice all the people down below. They look so small when you are up so high. What are the people down there doing I wonder? Maybe some are soldiers, all in armour. Perhaps we are in a castle from long ago, or one from a film or book? Maybe this is King Arthur's Castle and those are his knights? Perhaps there could be wizards there or magical creatures like unicorns? What can you see? Let your imagination paint the people and animals below. This is an imaginary castle after all, so anything you can dream of could be there! Let the carpet slowly circle around while you think of all the things that you can see. (Allow a few minutes for some creativity).

Now our carpet knows that we all need to start to head back to this room, so it begins to turn away from the castle to bring you back to the field where your adventure began. You can still see the birds flying around you, the blue sky and the fluffy clouds but now in the distance you see the green of the field. Your carpet begins to lower to the ground and finally it lands, very gently back on the grass. Wow, what an extraordinary trip that was. This magical carpet can take you anywhere, you just need to close your eyes and picture the carpet and anytime you need to go back to the castle or maybe somewhere new your imagination can take you there.

For now, we need to have a long stretch, breathing in take your arms over your head and stretch. Breath out and bring your arms back to your sides. Open your eyes, roll to one side and come back up to a sitting position.

8. Box of cares

You can just sit for this one; it is a lovely guided visualisation to do outside. If you can find somewhere really peaceful, even your own garden. Let's start by closing our eyes and taking in a breath and out, and again. We are going to imagine a beautiful box. This box can be small or large and it can be any colour you like, or maybe a mix of colours. Perhaps it has a special design you like or covered in a picture of your favourite super hero? Take a moment and think about what your box looks like. This box is going to be a very special box, one that is just for you. It has a lid, that only you can take off. This box is going to be your very own 'box of cares', you choose what you want to put into the box and also who you want to share the box with.

You can keep the box just to yourself, or you may like to share the box with someone, maybe your mum, dad, sister, brother, friend or teacher. Today we are going to think of something that we sometimes worry about. Perhaps you found a lesson a little hard today, or you had a fall out with one of your friends? It could be anything that you know has been on your mind, not just from today but from anytime. You are not going to worry about this thought, just let it pop into your head, don't think more about it, just take that thought and imagine popping it into your beautiful box.

Now close the lid on the box and the thought. You have taken it out of your mind and into your box. It is safe there but you no longer need to think about it. If sometime later you would like to share that thought with someone, you just need to picture your box and take out the thought. You can explain to the person you talk to that you have been able to put it into the box but would like to discuss it with them. Maybe after you do that, you will not need to put it into the box.

Or you might need to keep it in there for a while. Just know that when the thought is in the box, it will not keep popping into your head. You know where it is but it does not need to trouble you. Your box is there for any cares that pop in your head, at any time you can just open the lid and put them in there. Some may even stay there a long time; others may just go.

The box is just for you, so anytime you need it, you can just imagine it in your mind and it will appear. Now, let's put our boxes away. Just take a deep breath and imagine your box disappearing. (Don't worry you can picture it back anytime). Now take a deep breath in and stretch out those arms and legs, breath out and bring the arms back to your sides and open your eyes. Roll to one side and come up to sitting.

9. Time with Nature

I like doing this as a getting ready for bed Visualisation – so your child maybe in bed, or maybe after you have read a story you can just sit together as you go through it together. We are going to take a trip into a glorious park today, one that no one else visits. It is a beautiful sunny day, the sun is warm and there is a little breeze that brushes against our skin.

You feel comfortable and safe and looking around you see that you are on a path that leads to a river, follow that path until you get to the water's edge. Tied to a little jetty is a boat, this boat can fit as many people in as you need. Maybe you are taking this trip on your own, or perhaps you have a friend or family member with you. There could be lots of friends or even your pet! Choose if you would like to bring someone on this journey. Now step into the boat, it is very safe and does not even wobble.

This boat does not need anyone to row it, or steer it. It knows where it is going all by itself, so as you sit down it begins to slowly move away from the shoreline. Look around you as you start to move up the river. Can you hear the sounds of nature? The birds singing, the leaves rustling, the sound of the water against the side of the boat? What about what you see? The trees, hanging over the edge of the water, the fish in the river as you look over the side of the boat. Maybe there are birds fishing in the river, a heron or kingfisher? A fox coming down to drink or an otter swimming by the shore?

(Take a moments pause to allow them to form a picture. You can dangle your hand into the water, over the side of the boat. It is cool but refreshing and feels delicious against your skin. You can leave it in the water as your boat casually moves through the water. You are not in any hurry, you can just look around you and enjoy the motion of the boat and the sights and sounds of your journey. Think of all the colours that fill nature. The blue of the sky, the green, yellow and orange of the leaves of the trees. What about the river, is your river a particular colour?

Maybe a mix of lots of colours, or perfectly clear, so that you see right to the bottom? Looking around us every day allows us to see how amazing the world is. As we are always so busy, it is nice to just take a few moments and just appreciate where we are. Our boat is nearing the end of its journey and we see the shoreline coming up, where we can get back to land. So watch as your boat comes to shore, it is against another jetty where you can simply set out of the boat. You can take another moment to just look around you, feel the sun on your arms and face and think of how beautiful nature can be. Take a lovely breath in and out and then open your eyes, coming back to this room. Slowly roll to one side and come to sitting.

10. Tibetan Bowl

(You can use any chime, bell or even an app for the sound) You can have some really great Bell sounds recorded on these apps and as the aim is to really focus on a sound it does not matter if you do not have your own bowl or chimes. Though, they are lovely things to have in your home!

Getting into our comfy mindful position, either seated or lying down. We are going to close our eyes and take a breath in and out, and again. Today, we are going to use sound to really feel how our mind and our body is connected. When I start to create a note with the bowl I want you to place your hands on your tummy and think about how that sounds feels. (Hit the side of the bowl of circle around the edge to make the bowl sing. Do not talk while the sound is going). Could you feel the sound, even in your tummy? Were there other parts of you that felt the sound? Let's try that again (again with the bowl).

Notice if you felt the sound in a different place. Did the note seem to last longer or shorter? (Now play the bowl another way, hit, tap, sing but make the note either longer or shorter). How about this time? Did the note sound the same? Did you feel it in the same place as before? Can more of your body feel the sound? This time when I play the bowl I want you to think of a colour (play the bowl again). What colour was the sound for you? Was it a light gentle colour, or something loud and bold? If we do it again will you see the same colour? (Again play the bowl but change the note, loud too soft or short to long). How was the colour now? Was it the same as before? Was it just a different shade of the colour or had it completely changed?

Next time think about making that colour completely surround your body, as it you were put into a giant bubble filled with the colour. A safe bubble that can protect you, like a cloud, soft and gently. (Play the bowl) Allow the balloon of colour to work with the note, (you may need to tap the bowl again). Keep connecting the sound to the colour bubble.

Now as the note starts to fade, imagine your colour bubble also fading, gently like the note. When the note has finally finished you are back to normal breathing and your colour has gone. Take a moment before we open our eyes to think of the colour you pictured. Is it a colour you like? Would you choose that colour or did it just pop into your head? Was it bright or dark, bold or pastel? We don't need to overthink it, just take a moment to let yourself reflect on the colour. Now taking a breath in and out we are going to open our eyes. Roll to one side and come to sitting.

I hope that these scripted visualisations will provide you with a starting point. Many children and adults find that visualisations can really help them focus on their mindful practice. It can be hard to keep the mind 'quiet' and providing a focus throughout cannot only put aside this 'chatter' but also allow us to address specific needs. Techniques such as the box of cares and anxiety beach can harness mindfulness to provide tools to deal with situations and emotions that we can all face.

All of these exercises are suitable for all age groups, though the language has been written for the younger children. For children aged 9 and above I would recommend more mature language, though the techniques themselves are still extremely useful and are easily adapted for the older child. The power of visualisations can be felt at any age, so do not think that your tween will not 'get it'. Give one a go, and see what happens.

I have not written any 'follow up' exercises for these but it is a good idea to have time to reflect and return to every practice. It maybe that you only use one particular exercise with your child, just that you deepen the sessions. For many children and adults, it is the repeating of the practice that allows for a better understanding and therefore gain more benefits. They may choose a favourite that they are happy to hear again and again. You do not need to try them all, find the ones that you feel will work the best for your child or children and see how it develops. I am also constantly updating the website, so do check in and see what new material is there.

Mindful
Techniques

1.   Affirmations
2.   Kindness
3.   Mindful Stone
4.   Massage – Peer 2 Peer
5.   Massage – Self Massage
6.   The 5 Senses
7.   Chimes
8.   Gratitude
9.   Hand Mudras
10. Hand Mudra Affirmations
11. Body Scan
12. Mindful Jar
13. Affirmation Jar
14. Mindful Walking
15. Mindful Listening
16. Hand Affirmation
17. Affirmation Web
18. Thankful Lesson
19. Mindful Colouring
20. Mindful Wall

1. **Affirmations** I love affirmations! They are most probably my favourite thing to use with my own children. They hold amazing power and regardless of your child's age, there is always an affirmation you can use. These are positive words that your child can repeat. I have put some throughout this book and have downloadable lists available on the resources page at the end of the book. Simple phrases such as "I am kind", "I can do this" "I am loved" can work really well as a repeated phrase that children can remember and say to themselves.

These become Mantra's which are a great way to reinforce positive thoughts. Believing in the positive words that are spoken has a real effect on our brain. What we hear, we can believe. This can affect our image of how we perceive ourselves and how we think other perceive us.

Have a look at some of those in this book, or write some down with your child. You will see in this Chapter that Affirmations can be used in several ways.

2. Kindness – This has become the new 'buzz' word recently. However, often the point of the exercise is lost on the children. It can become a 'thing to do' or to gain some recognition for being 'kind.' The key to enabling our children to embrace kindness, is the simple act of doing something for someone, without expecting anything in return. An easy example is a compliment "your hair looks nice today", "I like your new shoes". We are not expecting a reply of 'yours does to' but maybe just a thank you. Kindness can become a rather large topic to discuss but it is one that if it is implemented simply, will give the children a wonderful tool. A great way of starting this at home would be a kindness circle. Sitting in a circle, every family member will say 1 kind thing to another. Once someone has had a kind thing said about them, they cannot be picked again. This can take a while to get going, but you often learn wonderful things about how the children perceive their family! You can also use this if you child is having any issues at school. If 1 child is being mean, or perhaps a relationship between friends has changed, ask them to think of 1 nice thing about that person. It can often just shift their thoughts from the present 'not nice' situation

3. Mindful Stones – These are natural rock crystals that are 'transformed' into 'magic' or 'mindful' stones. The key is to use a natural object, that is tactile and interesting. These can also form part of your 'Mindful Resources Kit' where you can make a project of having your own mindful objects – shells or personal collections that you encourage your children to gather. These can then stay at home and be used for many activities. We have included the Mindful Stones in a breathing activity but you can just as easily make it a discussion activity – pick a stone and discuss with a friend why you like your stone. Or how about mindful colouring? There are many different ways and the important part is that each child is able to choose their own stone. The engagement of selection is really vital to any additional work you then do.

4. Massage Each Other – Learning when it is appropriate to touch another person, and how that touch should feel, is an important aspect of our social world. With most Primary Schools following some form of 'touch policy' it can be extremely difficult for parents and children to

introduce a concept of 'positive touch'. I have tailored some simple ideas based on the well-known 'Story Time Massage Training' (I trained with the company) to enable you to bring some easy to use massage techniques into your home. A great favourite without having to learn too many techniques (all kids love it too) is the making a pizza massage!

Your child needs to be sat in-front of you with his/ her back towards you. You will discuss that you are going to be creating a Pizza Massage! It is essential before every massage to always ask permission. You need to ensure that your child is happy to be massaged and they understand the importance of asking another person if they are also happy to be massaged. This is all about trust and respect and teaching our children that asking someone first sets a clear boundary as to what is acceptable.

Now imagine you are going to knead your pizza dough – using both hands, gently form them into light fists and using the outside edge of your fist, pretend to knead the dough. You will always ask the person being massaged if it feels ok? If it is too hard then either stop or make your pressure less. Think of all the things that you would put onto a pizza and then imagine a way you can represent this with your hands. (I have put a full tutorial on the website – check out the resources page). So hands are light and you use only the fingertips for grated cheese, flat hand rolling across the back for putting on the tomato paste.

You get the idea, it is about having fun but also getting your child to feel another touch and learn how to massage a friend or family member and know what feels good. Not too heavy handed or fast. It really is a great way of getting our children to understand how touch can make you feel.

Give the ones you love wings to fly, roots to come back and reasons to stay

Dalai Lama

5. Massage – Self-Massage. For some children the ability to touch another child or in fact, to be touched will be too much. So let them participate but using their own body. They can make a mini pizza on their leg! It is just as important for them to feel the benefit of this positive touch.

6. The 5 Things – This is a great practice that you can take anywhere and use with any age. Name 5 things you can see, 4 things you can hear, 3 things you can touch, 2 things you can smell and 1 thing you can taste. It is a great way to really capture a Mindful Moment with your child. Opening up the senses to everything that is around you. I like doing this when we are out and about, maybe a park or even on the way to school.

7. Tibetan Chimes – These are simple metal disks that are connected via a strap. You tap one disk onto the other to create the 'chime.' Again, this works on vibrational sound and can be easy for any child to use. Both the bowl and the chimes can be used anywhere.

They also allow each child to actively participate, as they are so simple to use and depending on how the disks are 'tapped' depends on the volume and length of the sound. Both make for a great discussion afterwards.

NOTE; If your child has any sensory issues such as APD then have a quick practice of these or any other sound before you use it for a mindful practice. These are simple enough for even small children to use, they love making the sound and they are a great addition to any Mindful Toolbox.

Choose Kindness

Rachel Hawkes

8. Gratitude – Again a conceptual idea that is not often easy to broach. However, there are great ideas that children really embrace. You could start every day with 'what are you grateful for'. Explain that it does not always need to be the big things, a lovely home, or a holiday but often it is the small things – this attention is really the key to the exercise. They

may pick something that seems really small or even silly, such as 'I'm grateful I remembered my lunchbox' but it is the art of being aware that is so important.

Once a child is able to see that they are grateful for even small things then they are able to have a better awareness when the big events occur. This again takes time to build upon but it is well worth it. Taking only a couple of minutes at the start or end of the day it will get you all thinking. Alternatively, if you have more time or wish to make it a longer exercise you can create a 'jar of gratitude'. Or, a jar, box or even a list that they can mindfully decorate. A Gratitude Poster! There are many ideas that will come to you and them, but start small and try to incorporate into every day.

9. Hand Mudra – Providing a tool to help with focus is a great way of bringing mindfulness into the every-day for children and adults. Added into that a growing self-awareness and you have all the key ingredients for mindfulness – Hand Mudra's offer all!

It is the use of the hand to bring awareness, this exercise is suitable for all ages and works with the breath. In a relaxed seated position, start by taking their first finger and starting at the base of the thumb on the other hand they slowly slide the finger up the thumb (in breath), then down the other side (out breath), up the first finger (in breath) then down the other side (out breath). Repeat for each finger and then repeat on the other hand. It is worth demonstrating this first. They often have a unique way of performing the exercise! You can always use this when you are out and about. If your child is finding something difficult – maybe a large dog is barking or they go to an indoor playpark that is really noisy.

You can encourage them to use this practice at any moment. The joy of using hand mudras are that they come everywhere with us. Again, being able to just take a 'mindful moment'.

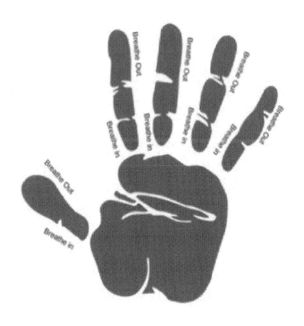

Breathe Out · Breathe In
Breathe Out · Breathe In
Breathe Out · Breathe In
Breathe Out · Breathe In
Breathe Out · Breathe In

10. Hand Mudra Affirmations – This is a little used gem that works really well with all ages. There are whole variety of these that can be used but a good one to start with is using a phrase of affirmation – it needs to only be 4 words as you will be using the fingers to say the affirmation.

One used in many yoga classes is 'peace begins with me', though also phrases such as 'I can do this', or 'I am thank-full' work too.

You can provide the affirmation or, you can have a separate time when they are able to make up their own. Once you have the phrase, you start in a sitting position and touch the thumb to the first finger, then second etc. saying each word of the affirmation as you touch the thumb to the finger. You can work with both hands at the same time or separately. As you can imagine not only can you use this anywhere but also at any time – so the 'I can do this' works well before exams or performances. There is a little video on website that will show you how to do it.

11. Body Scan – This brings the combination of body awareness and breath into a great centring exercise.

It works well with the children lying on the floor but can also be performed in a sitting position is necessary. Start with your basic position, lying comfortably with the eyes closed. Explain that you are going to take them on a journey through their body's and we are going to use the breath to focus on each part.

Starting at the toes, as you breath in scrunch up your toes as tight as you can, breath out and relax the toes, up to the calves (skip for KS1 if they do not know the body part), tighten the calves so that the feet lift off the ground, breath out and relax. Now the thighs, breath in, tighten, breath out, relax. Now the bottoms (they will always laugh), tense that bottom as you breath in, tight as you can, now breath out and relax. Tummies next, breath in and try to work those tummy muscles, breath out and relax… follow through the whole body.

When you get to the face ask them to close their mouths, clench the jaws together, then when they breath out, relax the jaw and have the mouth open just a little, with the tongue lose in the mouth. With the eyes, breath in and screw them tight shut, now breath out and relax, feel the eyes lightly behind the eyelids. Finish with this but let them just 'check in' to their body – how does it feel? Do you feel heavier against the floor? To finish get them all to breath in and take their arms overhead and the breath out and bring them back to their sides. Wiggle fingers and toes and then open the eyes.

12. Mindful Jar – What a great way of adding some creative play into the home. You will need a jar with a tight fitting lid, water, glitter and PVA glue.

There are various lovely videos on how to create this awesome mixture but simply, you get the kids to pour it all into a glass jar. The mindful aspect is in watching the medley of glitter swirl around until it settles at the bottom. Sounds simple but is very satisfying and children love them. Another variant is to create mood jars – they are the same as the mindful jar you just use different colours. Your child can then choose which jar they need to watch – sad, happy, lonely, friendly etc. You can discuss with them what emotion they think they need. Another great way of talking about emotions in an open and non-judgmental way, while providing them an outlet to explore this growing range of emotions.

13. Affirmation Jar – Another great family activity. Affirmations are a great tool to get children engaged and can be brought out at any time.

This activity relies on you either providing printed out affirmations (see our resources section) or getting your children to make their own. A combination of the two works very well. You will need time to explain an affirmation and how they can then write their own. You can always use topics that might be a topical for them, such as 'I am friendly', 'I am kind' 'I think of others', 'I will work hard'. If this is a family jar, then it is important that all members of the family are able to add something into the jar. Then every day, someone can pick from the jar – the affirmation can even go up on the wall and become the 'family affirmation of the day'. How you use it can always vary, getting the children to actively want to choose the affirmation daily is the important part. You can start each day with one for them, or even for the whole family. Or finish each day with choosing one from the jar. You can have one for the day, or week. A different one picked by each member of the family or a jar that is just for each child. Your options are endless and can change and be adapted as your children grow.

14. Mindful Walking – Sometimes in a busy day it is not always possible to 'plan' to create mindfulness. This is the joy of getting your children more 'aware' as we can take that moment of 'awareness' anywhere. So, think of a mindful walk. If you can do this outside that is perfect but if not and you are stuck inside on a cold, wet day just get the children to take off their shoes (and socks if able). Have a starting point and an end point, even if it is around the kitchen table. This is about connecting their feet to the ground, being aware of how this feels. So lifting one foot up, slowly place it in front of you, be aware that your heel touches first then the side

of your foot then your toes, now lift the next foot and notice how this one feels as it connects to the ground. What does the ground feel like? Is it cool, warm, soft, spikey... talk them through the experience. You can also bring in the breath, so as they breath-in lift the foot, breath-out as they place it on the ground. Hold the breath, breathe in lift the next foot, breath out place it down. When they are at the end they can either turn around and repeat or end with a calming breath in and out. This can bring about a great connection back to their own body and a sense of awareness of where their body is in relation to those around them and the environment. If you can do this outside – you can choose to walk on grass, or at the beach, it is all about finding the 'moment'.

15. Mindful Listening – Again this can be used in the home, outside or really anywhere you need it. In order to concentrate for this, they will need to be in a good starting position. You can be in a car, at home, out in the park. This is again about focusing on the Mindful Moment. Whether you are all seated or lying down? Try to have everyone with their eyes closed. Ask them, without speaking out loud what they can hear? Give it a few minutes, then ask them if they can hear anything outside of the room (if inside), How about any sounds that are near you? Or sounds that are further away? This is great for concentration and awareness. You can vary this by also getting them to discuss with you afterwards all the things they could hear.

16. Hand of Affirmation – This is a really fun activity that gets each child really focused on their own positive traits. Start with a piece of paper and ask the children to draw around their own hand. (Young children will need help with this) It needs to be their own hand as this is all about ownership – they then need to think of 5 positive things about themselves to write, one for each finger and their thumb onto their own Hand of Affirmation. Bring out the coloured pencils for this one. You can also make it more mindful by putting on some chilled music, or maybe taking them outside for a mindful walk before. Do not hurry with this one, it will take them time to think of things. They can then either cut these out and they can decorate a wall (see Mindful Wall later) or discuss with you and other family members. You can also come back to these for a discussion on another day – let them have the opportunity to speak about the positive things they have written. It is this reflection that is so crucial to embedding that positive self-image that we want all children to have. By taking time to reflect on what they have written, and also the time to create the hand, decorating it and cutting it out we ensure that they are taking real ownership of the words they have chosen.

17. Affirmation Web – Working still on our affirmations this is a seated activity where you can either print out a spider web (see the <u>Resources</u> Page) or alternatively your children can create their own. You just need to draw out a big spider web on a sheet of paper. It can have several webs, or layers a fit on an A4 sheet of paper or any size that you have at home. The children then can create Affirmations that they either write onto the web or cut out and stick onto the web. Again you can use pre-printed Affirmations or spend some time writing their own, or perhaps write some together. This can also be an ongoing project, starting with the inner web, they may add to the web throughout a day, week or weekend.

18. **Thankful Lesson** This is an exercise that you can do at any time but it is a great one for getting your child to really think. Ask them what they are 'Thankful' for today? This can just be a fun 5-minute discussion or you may want to take more time and ask them to write it down. You can do this why waiting in a que at the shops, driving to a club or eating a picnic with friends. There is no right or wrong, they do not have to think of 10 things, just get them thinking. It will hopefully spark lots of chatting. You can all discuss this together or just keep it light – again it is an opportunity for a Mindful Moment. How long you spend is up to you.

I am Perfectly Imperfect

19. Mindful Colouring – Possibly the best known of the 'mindful activities'. This is the simple pleasure of just focusing on colouring in. To make the activity really special you may want to use Mandalas (see Resources List) and explain to your children that this special pattern reflects the universe, our planet and our place on that planet. There are some beautiful Mandalas available for colouring in and again it would be advisable to have a selection available to that each child can pick their own design to decorate. I have put a small selection on the website that you can download. Children are able to embrace the joy of such a simple activity without the need to worry about patterns, exact colour, what is the right way, or what someone else may do. Do not underestimate the joy of a box of lovely coloured pencils and the time and space to just enjoy creativity. You can have a picture that they come back to, or a fresh one each time. Choice is part of the process. You can spend 5 minutes or a whole morning! The pictures can then form part of your Mindful Wall...

20. Mindful Wall – With these Mindful Moments that you and your children are spending, how about – creating an area to be show your family and friends? You could make some space and let them create a 'mindful wall'? It can encompass their; mindful colouring, affirmations, words of gratitude, hand affirmations or just photos of them when they have been enjoying themselves. A place in your home that is all about celebrating the mindful moments!

End of Every Session

I would recommend that you spend between 3-10 minutes of talking time at the end of every Mindful session. This time is really does allow your child time to process the activity. Creating a time 'together' to either reflect or discuss the practice, is sometimes the best part. You can really work on your connection to each other and they feel listened too and their opinion valued.

It is important that your child feels 'part' of this practice, even if for some of the exercises they are working alone, it brings you together at the end. These Mindful Moments are for you to share, though hopefully they will start to use some of these tools in other situations too.

I always end with a bow and either a "namaste' or 'thank you' to everyone. This is just an addition I like to add but it does bring in a great sense of gratitude of the time shared together.

How are you going to set your Intent for after the session? You can perhaps discuss an activity you could do at another practice; or maybe bringing a friend or another family member into some of the sessions. Let your child lead you with this. Sometimes they are just done, other times they will want to chat away about ideas! Glitter in a mindful jar or what affirmations they could draw, a mandala they would like to colour in. These are often the best "mindful moments', when you give your child the time and space to let their brain take them where it wants to go.

Maybe you can take elements out of sessions to discuss? On the school run you could ask: that …… worked really well yesterday how about we try that before homework tomorrow?

Do you think we can add .... into our bedtime tonight?

Active engagement is one of the main benefits of this time. Throw out a question and see what happens? Embrace the creativity that always comes with Mindfulness with children. They will take you on a path that you never even thought about!

 Don't forget – this is meant to be fun!

Bring it Together

The practices in this book are all about you finding the time to come together and learn and develop. The idea is not to be hung up on the right position or technique but to find time to connect with your children.

Be aware of the things that you do as a family. Yes, we are busy and we need to teach our children how to empty the dishwasher and learn their times tables but there is also space for the skills of respect, consideration, trust, empathy and the emotions of happiness, joy and contentment.

I hope that this book will show you some simple pointers of how you can engage with your child and feel that connection, that will last a lifetime.

Resources List

If you want to put together your own Mindful Toolbox then I have listed below some items that I use in classes and with my own children. Links to my FREE resources are all via the Website, all other items are via Amazon, where I do have an affiliate link – which does provide a small commission, though not enough to feed the rabbit! Check out www.buddhabuddies.co.uk/resources for easy links to all these items

- Music – this can be something chilled that you are all familiar with or perhaps you can all choose some music together. Ambient music works well.
- Mandala's – There are free Mandala pintable's available on the Buddha Buddies Website
- Affirmations – I have created some PDF's that are free to

download on the <u>website</u>. Though you can always make up your own!

- The Massage each other video is also found on the <u>resources</u> page.
- <u>Hoberman Sphere</u> – Good old Amazon is great for these. I would recommend buying a good one, the cheap ones just break.
- Colour Scarfs – I like the ones from Amazon but you can just as easily cut up some old ones you no longer use.
- <u>Mindful Stones</u> – You can just have some that you collect or you can also often pick up lovely ones at museums. The link is to a lovely large collection of lots of different ones.
- <u>Eye Pillows</u> – You can happily make your own eye pillows. There

are plenty of YouTube videos, or purchase some lovely ones from Online

- <u>Tibetan Singing Bowl</u> – These are an investment, though kids love them and they will of course last a lifetime
- <u>Tibetan Chimes</u> – Again, these are very kid friendly and bring an element that is unique to any practice.
- <u>Feathers</u> – Simple but still effective.
- Empty Jars – Just wash and then ready to go
- Coloured Crayons/ Pencils/ Paper
- <u>Balloons</u> – I love using a range of colours. These ones are great
- Seasonal Objects (Flowers/ Autumn Leaves etc) – just have a

look in your garden or on the way to school.

- <u>Bubbles</u> – if you can get a small bubble machine, they are still great fun for all ages.

Books, Articles, Websites and Links

There are so many books, apps, articles, blogs and research out there. I've put together my favourites for some delving if you would like to look into Mindfulness for you and your children further.

Books

'Sitting still like a frog' by Eline Snel 2013

'Connected Kids' by Lorraine E. Murray 2014

The Science of Meditation by Daniel Goldman & Richard J. Davidson 2017

Roots and Wings. Every childhood needs a revolution: A Handbook for Parents and Educators. By Alex Koster 2018

The Dalai Lama's Book Of Wisdom by Dalai Lama 2012

Apps

I know that there is lots of snobbery regarding the nature of using an App to meditate or practice mindfulness. Personally, I love a good one. They remind me that it is the accessibility that is important.

Insight Timer – My App of choice. Perfect for a sense of connection to others and the variety of high quality content.

The Gratitude App – Sounds strange but it pops a little reminder to you every day to think about something you are grateful for. I love it!

Research & Articles

There are some great links to research on the resource page. Links to some great ones can be found on the resources page on the Buddha Buddies Website

Blogs on Mindful Parenting

GAIM
https://www.gaiam.com/blogs/disco ver/how-to-become-a-mindful-parent

Websites

Buddha Buddies
www.buddhabuddies.co.uk
For details on Baby Yoga and Massage Classes in the UK and a great resource for downloads and blogs relating to Mindfulness for Parents and Children.

BBEd
www.bbed.org.uk
Providing courses for Primary School Educators looking to introduce Yoga & Mindfulness into the main curriculum

Cosmic Kids
www.cosmickids.com/tag/mindful-parenting/
A fab online resource for parents on yoga and mindfulness

Left Brain Buddha
https://leftbrainbuddha.com

Offering lots of advice and support for parents looking to be mindful.

Nourish To Thrive
www.nourishtothrive.co.uk
A great website for Mums who need any Post-Natal Support with tips and blogs. I love their Nourished Mum Cards. Perfect for Mindful Moments for parents.

Chilled out Child
https://chilledoutchild.com
If you want to take your Mindfulness with children further – they provide amazing training on how to become a Children's Mindfulness Teacher.

Mindful. Org – magazine and website
A source of blogs, research, tips and generally everything mindful related

Story Time Massage

www.storymassage.co.uk

If you would like to know more about learning peer-to-peer massage they are brilliant.

10 of Zen

www.10ofzen.com/welcometothelibrary

A great website and resource for parents looking for 10-minute meditations to add into their day.

Big Thanks
And
Namaste

I would like to thank many people who in many ways have inspired or helped me get to this point. Although I have been practicing Mindfulness for several years, it is the imparting of a tiny bit of this skill that has made me really see its true power.

To Heidi M Illustrates for her amazing characters which brought this book to life for me. Jo Beer for creating my wonderful book cover. Sharon Denney for our love of rabbit holes.

Claire Mitchel at The Girls Mean Business, who gave the best masterclass on how to self-publish (convincing me I could really do this). To all the Buddha Buddies Mummies who put up with my crazy mindful moments at the end of our classes. To my brother Paul Hawkes, Thanks for the time to edit and giving me some awesome ideas! Also to Georgie Cassas and Hannah Carr great editors, your thoughts and kind comments have made this much tidier!

Most of all my beautiful daughters, Bella & Mia who show me how I need to be aware of our 'Mindful Moments.' You are more precious to me with every day. This one is for you!

And breath

x

Rachel

It would be great to hear what you think of the book, so please do leave a review over on Amazon. You can also contact Rachel direct via her Instagram Account @rachelhawkes

About the Author

Rachel is a mother of two girls and likes to wear several hats! Graduate of Liverpool University with a combined honours degree in English & Psychology. She started off in the corporate world of sales and marketing. Taking the leap into the holistic world in 2005 when she trained as a Massage Therapist.

Since then she has had twin girls, set up a Holistic Wellbeing Centre and established a Baby & Children's Yoga Business. She runs between teaching and massaging with the balance of family life thrown in too!

Qualified in various Massage techniques, Kids Yoga and Mindfulness and a long term meditator, she is a self-confessed 'life-long learner'.

Passionate about the balance between enabling our children to be both kind and resilient, she works with families and schools to ensure that the skills of mindfulness are embedded into the next generation at every opportunity.

This is her first foray into publishing and has freely admitted it has been a 'very scary process'!

Printed in Poland
by Amazon Fulfillment
Poland Sp. z o.o., Wrocław